Kensuke's Kingdom

BY MICHAEL MORPURGO

BOOK ANALYSIS

Written by Jeremy Lambert and Tina Van Roeyen
Translated by Emma Hanna

Kensuke's Kingdom
BY MICHAEL MORPURGO

Bright
≡Summaries.com

MICHAEL MORPURGO

BRITISH NOVELIST

- **Born in St Albans (England) in 1943.**
- **Notable works:**
  - *War Horse* (1982), children's novel
  - *Arthur, High King of Britain* (1994), children's novel
  - *Private Peaceful* (2003), children's novel

Michael Morpurgo originally intended to join the British Army, but decided to abandon his training in favour of teaching English in Kent. He discovered his talents as a storyteller one day when, seeing that his pupils were bored by their assigned reading, he decided to make up some stories of his own to tell them. His students' positive feedback encouraged him to submit these stories to a publisher, and his first majorly successful novel, *War Horse*, was published when he was just shy of his 40th birthday.

Following the success of *War Horse*, he decided to resign from his job and become a full-time writer, while also devoting himself to helping children from troubled backgrounds: for many years, he and his wife Clare have organised visits for underprivileged children to the farm they own. He has received many awards both for his contributions to literature and for his social activism, and has garnered a great deal of global recognition for his work. Several of his books have been adapted for the cinema, including *War Horse* (2011), which was directed by Steven Spielberg (American producer, screenwriter and director, born in 1946).

KENSUKE'S KINGDOM

FRIENDSHIP FOUND IN THE UNLIKELIEST OF PLACES

- **Genre:** adventure novel
- **Reference edition:** Morpurgo, M. (2003) *Kensuke's Kingdom*. New York: Scholastic Press.
- **1st edition:** 1999
- **Themes:** adventure, friendship, solitude, nature, robinsonade

Kensuke's Kingdom is a first-person adventure told from the perspective of Michael, a British teenager whose parents decide to sail around the world after losing their jobs. However, one night Michael and his dog, Stella Artois, venture onto the deck of the sailboat during a storm and they are both swept overboard. They wake up on a deserted beach and try to survive as best they can, and it is not long before Michael crosses paths with the island's sole inhabitant: Kensuke, an elderly Japanese man who was stranded there 40 years ago. The old man begins teaching Michael how to survive in the wilderness, and the two overcome their differences to forge a strong bond.

In 2000, a jury of 20 000 children voted *Kensuke's Kingdom* the winner of the Children's Book Award for that year.

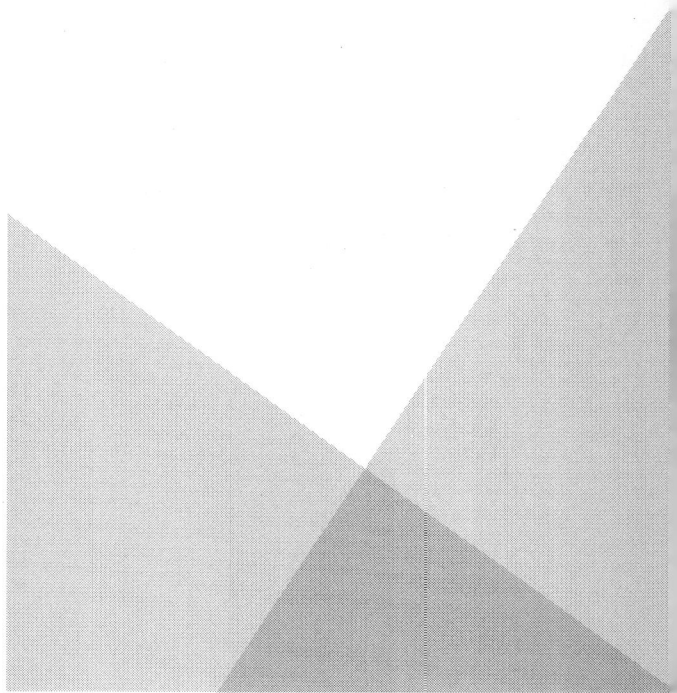

SUMMARY

In the late 1990s, a British man named Michael, who is the novel's narrator and protagonist, begins writing down the story of an adventure he had while sailing around the world many years ago, in which he and his dog were shipwrecked on an island whose only other inhabitant was a man named Kensuke.

After forging a strong friendship with Kensuke and finding a way to leave the island, Michael made his companion a promise, which he has kept: to wait ten years before telling anyone about the island's existence so that Kensuke can live out his life in peace. Now that this time has passed, Michael has decided to put pen to paper and tell the story of how he met Kensuke.

THE START OF A GREAT ADVENTURE

Until Michael turns 11, "life [is] just normal" (p. 2): he enjoys playing football with his friends, especially Eddie Dodds, his "best friend in all the world" (p. 3), and every Sunday his parents take him and their beloved dog, Stella Artois, to an artificial lake where his parents can indulge their passion for sailing. Fishing and spending time lounging around on the family boat is their special tradition.

However, one day his parents receive a letter telling them that they have been laid off. His father, who believes that there are no job opportunities in the area they are living in, disappears for an entire week before telling the rest of the family to meet him in a seaside town. When they arrive, he shows them the *Peggy Sue*, a sailboat which he wants to take on a trip around the world with them. Over the next months, Michael's mother studies and gets a Yachtmaster's certificate, enabling her to act as skipper for the journey, and the family sets off on 10 September 1987. Eddie Dodds comes to see them off, and throws Michael a football as a farewell gift, saying that it will bring him good luck on his travels.

Although their journey goes smoothly, it is still thrilling and highly educational. Michael keeps a journal in which he records all of his thoughts and feelings about his experiences and the aspects of the natural world he has discovered.

The family makes stops in the Canary Islands, South Africa, Brazil and Australia, but on the eve of Michael's 12ᵗʰ birthday, the *Peggy Sue* is caught in a storm while en route to Papua New Guinea. Michael climbs on deck in search of Stella Artois while the storm is raging and sees that she has fallen overboard. When he attempts to rescue her, he is also swept into the roiling waves of the Pacific Ocean.

A LOST ISLAND

Michael is buffeted back and forth by the waves, clinging to his football like a lifebelt. However, his strength soon runs out and he falls unconscious. When he wakes up, he finds himself on a beach with no one but his dog for company.

The island they have washed up on is "two or three miles in length, no more" (p. 49), and is covered in trees inhabited by screeching monkeys, but seems to be otherwise deserted. In spite of the hopelessness of their situation (as Michael realises that, for example, it will be difficult to find fresh water), he gradually starts hoping that he will eventually be reunited with his parents.

As hunger and thirst begin to set in, Michael and Stella seek shelter in a cave for the night. When Michael wakes up the next morning, he finds that Stella has disappeared. He finds her just as she is about to start eating a raw fish and some bananas, which have mysteriously appeared a short distance away from the cave they slept in. Michael takes this to mean that someone is watching over them, and shouts "Thank you!" into the distance three times (p. 59).

The next day, Michael decides to flag down one of the ships that occasionally pass by the island, and starts a fire by using a shard of glass to create a concentrated beam of sunlight. When he comes back from gathering more wood to feed the fire with, he discovers someone he initially mistakes for an orangutan stamping out the flames. However, it turns out to be an old man, who introduces himself as Kensuke. He seems very angry, which frightens Michael, but Stella "greet[s] him like a long lost friend" (p. 67). Kensuke then divides the island into two areas: one for himself, and one for Michael, whom he orders never to light a fire again.

Although Kensuke wishes to preserve his solitary way of life, away from the hustle and bustle of society, he knows that Michael is alone and struggling to survive. He therefore brings him various bits of food each day.

When Michael spots another ship cresting the horizon, he is faced with a dilemma: should he disobey Kensuke's orders and light a fire to attract its attention, or let it continue on its way, at the risk of being stranded on the island forever? As Michael says, "the old man [...] was looking after me, he was keeping me alive, but he was also keeping me prisoner" (p. 83).

His esteem for his protector is diminished somewhat when Kensuke forbids him to bathe after a long storm, and then destroys the lighthouse Michael has built to signal to any passing ships. As usual, the old man appears, yells at him in Japanese and then disappears as soon as the boy acquiesces to his demands. However, this time Michael is so exasperated that he decides to defy Kensuke's orders, and goes to bathe anyway. This proves to be a mistake when he is stung by jellyfish and falls unconscious.

KENSUKE'S FRIENDSHIP

Michael wakes up in Kensuke's cave, paralysed by the jellyfish poison. Kensuke is looking after him, and Michael begins paying close attention to his orderly way of life while he recovers. In particular, he learns how to find food, to preserve what he finds and even to paint shells, which is Kensuke's great passion.

In the next chapter, Kensuke reveals a bit about himself: he tells Michael that his hometown, Nagasaki, was destroyed by the atom bomb that was dropped on it by American forces. He escaped the bombing because he had already been shipwrecked on the island, where he wishes to stay. This is partially because he wants to escape from the destructiveness of humanity, and partially because he believes that his wife and child were killed in the bombing.

Once Michael and Kensuke have built up some mutual trust, they become very close friends. However, Michael misses his family, and throws a message in a bottle into the ocean without telling Kensuke that he has done so. Unfortunately, the bottle washes up on the island again the next day, and Kensuke finds it. He does not reproach Michael, but simply starts avoiding him, and Michael "grieve[s] for [his] lost friendship" (p. 130).

However, Kensuke's protective side soon resurfaces, and he decides to help Michael build a lighthouse that would enable him to flag down a ship. The two friends soon get swept up in their enthusiasm for their task, and Kensuke even begins to imagine leaving the island and returning to Japan, where he could search for his wife and son. However, this excitement quickly dissipates when a group of poachers lands on the island, to Kensuke's great alarm.

When another boat appears on the horizon, Kensuke is initially wary, but he eventually permits Michael to light a massive fire. The boat approaches, and Michael is overcome with joy when he realises that it is the *Peggy Sue*. To his great surprise, Kensuke refuses to leave the island with him, and the old man asks him to promise him three things:

- to paint something every day for the rest of his life;
- to think of him at every full moon;

- to never speak of the island for the next ten years.

Once they have said a tearful goodbye, Michael leaves his old friend's side for good to return to his parents.

Ten years have gone by, and he has decided to publish the story. After reading the book, Kensuke's son Michiya writes to Michael to tell him that, contrary to the old man's belief, he and his mother survived the bomb, and that their family was delighted to learn that Kensuke had not died when his ship sank. Finally, Michiya tells Michael that he would love to meet him.

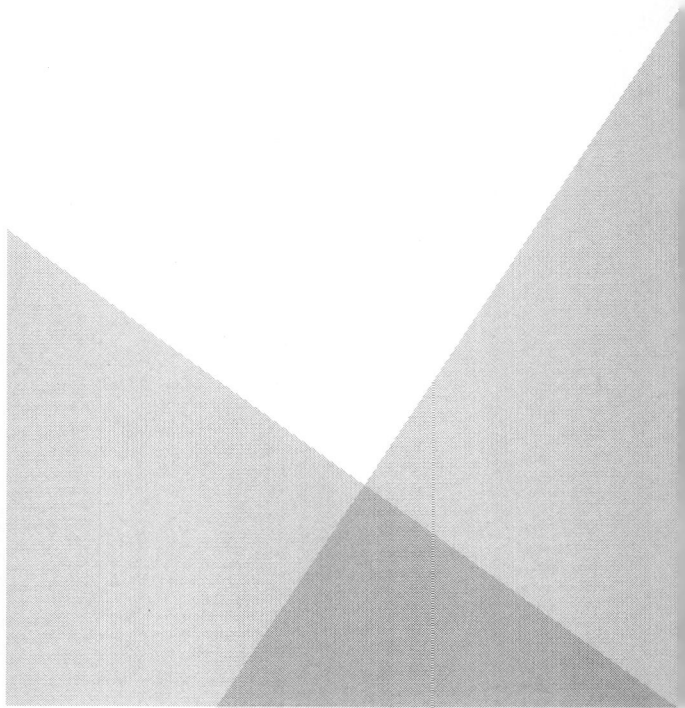

CHARACTER STUDY

MICHAEL

Michael is the narrator of the story. He is a young boy who is just shy of his teenage years, and is presented as a generous, respectful, humble individual. These qualities have given him a knack for making friends easily. Since the story is told in the first person, his physical appearance is not described in detail, although we are told that he enjoys playing football, particularly with his best friend Eddie Dodds.

In the novel, Michael is telling the story of an adventure he had ten years earlier. During his time aboard the *Peggy Sue*, he keeps a journal in which he describes his interest in nature and natural phenomena, which plays a direct role in the way he learns about the wonders of the world around him: "I still dream of the elephants in South Africa. I loved how slow they are, and thoughtful [...] I think I'm happier than I have ever been in my life" (p. 34).

Furthermore, this journal and the knowledge he has amassed in it form the basis of the novel he writes ten years later. Michael also learns how to sail thanks to his mother's lessons, as well as how to use squid ink as paint, how to smoke a fish, and many other useful skills. He finds it easy to adapt in the face of difficult circumstances and is shown to be adept at solving problems.

DR KENSUKE OGAWA

Even though the book is named after him, Kensuke does not appear until the fifth of the novel's ten chapters, and his life story is not revealed until much later, which shrouds him in a certain degree of mystery:

> "He was diminutive, no taller than me, and as old a man as I had ever seen. He wore nothing but a pair of tattered breeches bunched at the waist, and there was a large knife in his belt. He was thin, too. In places – under his arms, around his neck, and his midriff – his copper-brown skin lay in folds about him, almost as if he'd shrunk inside it. What little hair he had on his head and his chin was long and wispy and white." (p. 66)

Kensuke is from Nagasaki in Japan, and is a trained gynaecologist. He and his wife Kimi have a son called Michiya. When the Second World War (1939-1945) broke out, he enlisted in the navy, but was shipwrecked on the island after his ship was destroyed during a naval battle. While the ship's radio was still functioning, he heard a report saying that an atomic bomb had been dropped on his hometown, which convinced him that he was better off staying on the island forever in order to escape the cruelty of humanity.

On the island, he is able to live in harmony with nature and spend his time painting and fishing. Over the decades he has spent there, he has established a routine that suits him perfectly: he cleans, hunts and spends several hours each day painting Japanese trees and animals. This pastime keeps his connection to his homeland alive, and also helps him to bond with Michael when he passes this skill on to him.

Kensuke's feelings towards Michael evolve from distrust to fondness over time. He teaches Michael everything he knows and the boy becomes his only friend, in spite of the old man's almost selfish desire for privacy. He is cautious and thoughtful by nature, and eventually admits that Michael would be better off with his family. He therefore helps him to find a way of leaving the island, returning to his solitude and proving the sincerity of his friendship once and for all.

STELLA ARTOIS

Stella is Michael's dog, and is described as a "black-and-white sheepdog, who always seem[s] to know what [is] about to happen" (p. 2). She proves herself to be a faithful, considerate companion both on the sailboat and on the island that she and her master are washed up on. She accompanies Michael on all of his adventures, and often provides him with invaluable aid: for example, she finds the food that Kensuke has left for them, and her welcoming attitude helps him to realise that they have nothing to fear from Kensuke.

MICHAEL'S PARENTS

Michael's parents both work at a brickworks and have a passion for sailing: their favourite way of escaping the humdrum of their everyday lives is to spend their Sundays sailing on an artificial lake. One day, his mother even says, "This is how life is supposed to be. Wonderful, just wonderful" (p. 4).

His father is the one who suggests sailing around the world, which is a dream he has harboured for years. When life takes a turn for the unexpected, he takes advantage of this opportunity and uses it to get his wife on board with this plan and make his dream come true. All they need to do is wait six months while Michael's mother completes a brief but intense period of training to become a licensed skipper!

During their time on the sailboat, Michael's parents display great bravery, perseverance and determination. They pay attention to their son and entrust him with a great deal of responsibility, as well as constantly searching for new ways to enrich his education. They also display that bravery and determination anew by spending more than a year searching tirelessly for their son.

ANALYSIS

A BLEND OF REALISM AND ADVENTURE

Kensuke's Kingdom uses first-person narration, which usually implies that the events of the story are being recounted by the protagonist-narrator as they happen. In other words, it is assumed that the narrator does not know what is going to happen next, which makes the story seem more exciting and adventurous, especially when it is set in an exotic location like in this book.

However, this book is also written in the past tense, and is framed as the protagonist, Michael, revisiting the events of his past after ten years have gone by. While the novel still maintains a degree of suspense throughout, it is usually more closely related to the twists and turns of the story than to its ending, which is revealed in the first few lines of the book.

Furthermore, excerpts from the journal that Michael kept during his time on the ship are scattered through the book, and serve as evidence that the voyage really happened, as they back up Michael's story of being swept overboard.

This narrative strategy allows the author to make the novel seem more like a true story than a work of fiction, which makes the adventures it contains seem even more exciting and realistic.

THE THEME OF FRIENDSHIP

The novel depicts friendship as a strong bond between two individuals who know that they can always rely on each other, no matter how much physical distance separates them. The character of Michael is the common factor in all of the many friendships depicted in the novel, with three different relationships being the most significant:

- **The relationship between Michael and Stella Artois.**
  Stella Artois symbolises unconditional loyalty, as she protects Michael, warns him of danger and always obeys him. She is also his playmate, and her high spirits are never dampened. It is actually because of Michael's worry for Stella that he falls overboard in the first place, and

they are left clinging to each other as they are swept away, creating a powerfully symbolic image. During their time on the island, Stella acts as a source of optimism and entertainment for Michael, and she also helps him and Kensuke take the first steps towards becoming friends.

- **The relationship between Michael and Eddie Dodds.**
  Although Eddie is not physically present on the island, Michael often thinks about him while he is stranded there. For example, when Michael is trying to light a fire, he remembers Eddie explaining that shards of glass can be used to do so, which allows him to solve this problem. Furthermore, Eddie is symbolically present throughout the entire story through the football he gives Michael as a present. This ball becomes "a sort of talisman for [Michael], a lucky charm, and it really seemed to work, too" (p. 21), and it never leaves the protagonist's side through all his adventures on the boat, in the ocean and on the island. This also gives him a tangible reminder of his homeland and spurs him to keep looking for a way to get back to his family. It even saves his life, as Michael

is able to cling to the football and stay afloat in the middle of the ocean without exhausting himself when he is swept overboard. In a scene laden with symbolism later in the book, Kensuke gives the football back to Michael after they become friends, after having initially hidden it elsewhere on the island.

- **The relationship between Michael and Kensuke.**
Michael's relationship with Kensuke gets off to a rocky start, as the old man initially treats Michael very coldly. However, Stella Artois acts as an intermediary between the two and is able to bring them together. Their friendship is a constant work in progress, and is largely based on an exchange of knowledge: for example, Kensuke teaches Michael how to paint, and learns English from him. Although their relationship is quite complicated, the two protagonists are able to overcome their differences by making an effort to forgive and understand each other: as Michael says, "We were happy, and I was his family" (p. 124), which is echoed by Kensuke saying "You are like son to me now" (*ibid.*). However, Kensuke's paternal attitude towards

Michael becomes increasingly possessive over time, and he even asks Michael not to try to leave the island, as it would be too devastating for him. Kensuke's broad distrust of humanity means that it takes him a while to fully accept Michael's presence in his life, and he does not want his young friend to draw anyone else's attention to the island, as this would threaten his peaceful way of life. However, as they become closer friends, the old man eventually decides to help Michael return to his family so that he can be happy. Finally, it is worth noting that the novel opens with Michael revealing that he promised Kensuke that he would not divulge his identity or the secret of the island's existence for ten years. He has kept that promise, which is further proof of their friendship.

There are also a number of other friendships that are explored in the novel in lesser detail, such as the bond between Michael and his father ("My father became my friend, my shipmate. We came to rely on each other", p. 15) and the friendship between Kensuke and the orangutan Tomodachi, whom he treats like a member of the family.

A CLASSIC SETTING FOR AN ADVENTURE NOVEL

Uninhabited islands are a staple of adventure novels, and instantly bring to mind classic works such as *Robinson Crusoe* (1719) by Daniel Defoe (English writer, 1660-1731) and *Treasure Island* (1883) by Robert Louis Stevenson (1850-1894) – or maybe even *Lord of the Flies* (1954) by William Golding (British writer, 1911-1993), albeit with rather different connotations!

This sub-genre of adventure fiction has been dubbed the "robinsonade", and is based on two key themes: isolation, and the loss of all connections (to family, society, everyday life, nature, and so on).

In general, the protagonists of these novels find themselves stranded on a desert island and have to find a way to survive. Although they are seeking a way to return to normality, their adventure leaves an indelible mark on them, and when they eventually manage to return to their normal lives they find that nothing is quite the same as it was before.

In other words, the robinsonade depicts an interval in the protagonist's life in which all the rules that govern their existence are turned on their head, often forcing them to reconnect with nature. This distance from society often allows the characters to see it more clearly and become more conscious of its flaws.

Kensuke's Kingdom follows this pattern, as Michael is left stranded on an island, separated from his family and with no idea of what has happened to them, and has to learn how to live in harmony with nature. This allows him to learn about animals such as orangutans, monkeys and tortoises, and he makes a new friend in Kensuke.

Most of the book's social criticism is embodied by the character of Kensuke, particularly through his desire to put as much distance as possible between himself and the rest of society, not to mention the wars and destruction it brings.

However, this criticism is tempered with optimism, and the book ends on a positive note: Michael's decision to return to the United Kingdom could be interpreted as a desire to give civilisation another chance – without forgetting the lessons he has learned from nature – and the novel ends with the discovery that Kensuke's family survived the war and the atrocities that were committed during it.

FINDING A HOME IN NATURE

Before the storm

Nature often plays a key role in adventure novels, whether as a helper, an obstacle, or simply a backdrop.

The idea of nature is evoked before the family has even left England when Michael's father describes Michael's school as "the monkey school" (p. 2), because "the children gibbered and screeched and hung upside down on the jungle gym" (*ibid.*), and he affectionately refers to Michael as "monkey face" (*ibid.*). Outdoor sports such as football and mountain biking are also mentioned early in the novel, but sailing and everything associated with it (the feeling of the wind in your hair, speed, freedom, unpredictability, fishing) takes centre stage. When Michael's parents are laid off, his father decides to go to a seaside town on the south coast of England, where he finds the *Peggy*

Sue – a sailboat that becomes the family's new home and their means of making their dream to sail around the world a reality. Although some characters, such as Michael's grandmother, see nature – and, by extension, adventure – as something to be feared ("Icebergs, hurricanes, pirates, whales, supertankers, freak waves", p. 13), even she changes her mind when she sees her family boarding the ship, and expresses her desire to "see koalas in the wild" (p. 16).

Nature also provides an opportunity for Michael to learn new skills, such as navigating using a sextant, a compass and the position of the stars and keeping a journal (which allows him to discover a latent passion for writing: "I found I didn't really write it down at all. Rather, I said it" (p. 23). His father also predicts "he'll learn more in a couple of years at sea than he ever would in that monkey school of his" (p. 12).

Nature's ambivalence: both friend and foe

The book's descriptions of nature begin to change from Chapter 4 onwards: vast stretches of white sand, dense forests and lush vegetation are the first things Michael sees when he wakes up on the island. Although the visual descriptions of the island are complemented by aural descriptions, Morpurgo chiefly appeals to the reader's sense of sight: "Birds cackled and screeched high above me, and always the howling wailed and wafted through the trees, but more distantly now. It wasn't the sounds of the forest that bothered me, though, it was the eyes. I felt as if I were being watched by a thousand inquisitive eyes" (p. 48).

Morpurgo's description of the island matches up perfectly with the classic imagery associated with desert islands (dense vegetation, scorching heat, ocean waves stretching as far as the eye can see), and does not really deviate from this norm. Furthermore, Michael is overawed by it: "I remember thinking how wonderful it was, a green jewel of an island framed in white, the sea all around it a silken shimmering blue" (p. 50).

After initially marvelling at the stunning vistas before him, the young protagonist realises that the island is "bereft of all edible vegetation" (p. 52), and one problem after another arises after that: the trees are too tall, smooth and thin for Michael to climb them and pick their fruit, and he cannot find any fresh water. Having been momentarily transfixed by the beauty of nature, he then comes to the realisation that it is wild and untameable: "The forest became impenetrable at this point, dark and menacing" (p. 53), and the mosquitoes buzzing incessantly around him make him feel as though he is going mad. However, the island is also a source of lifesaving natural resources, including the fish and red bananas left for him by Kensuke.

Nature can therefore be described as an indifferent, unpredictable force, as it can act as both friend and foe to the characters. For example, sunlight keeps insects at bay, but can also cause sunburn, and fierce storms blow over as quickly as they appear. Finally, the sparkling sea seems like the perfect place for a leisurely swim – one of the few pastimes Michael is able to indulge in on the island – but its welcoming appearance belies the danger posed by the jellyfish lurking below the waves.

A special bond

Kensuke has spent 40 years on the island, which has enabled him to learn all of its secrets and forge a harmonious relationship with its flora and fauna. The cave he calls home is decorated with herbs, dried flowers, shells and bamboo, and he makes his own boats, never letting anything go to waste – he even uses squid ink to paint with and orangutan hair for his paintbrushes. Kensuke's wisdom has all been learned through experience: he knows where and when to hide, how to solve problems, and "seemed to have found ways to satisfy his every need" (p. 110).

Many different kinds of animals live on this tropical island, and Kensuke has formed a particularly close bond with a group of around 20 orangutans, including their offspring, which keep him company. He has given each of them a name to tell them apart (naturally, these names are Japanese in origin, such as Tomodachi and Kikanbo). These orangutans are more than just secondary characters: they are Kensuke's adopted family, and have taught him a great deal:

> "He learned he said mostly by watching what the orangutans ate, and what they did not eat. He learned to climb as they did. He learned to understand their language, to heed their warning signals [...] Slowly he built a bond of trust and became one of them." (p. 121)

He is also inspired by the bravery of the turtles:

> "They do not know what they find out there, what happen to them; but they go, anyway. Very brave. Maybe they teach me good lesson. I make up my mind. When one day ship come, and we light fire, and they find us, then I go. Like turtles I go." (pp. 142-143)

Kensuke's friendship with the orangutans shows that people cannot live without companionship, and need relationships (even if they are with animals) to survive. Kensuke and the orangutans eventually become mutually dependant on each other, and in the end he refuses to leave the island because of them, knowing that they would fall prey to poachers if he left.

A COMING-OF-AGE NOVEL

Michael has two adventures that change his life forever: the trip around the world on the sailboat with his parents, and the year he spends stranded on the desert island with Kensuke.

At the start of the novel, Michael is just a typical pre-teen boy whose most pressing thoughts are about football. However, over the course of his extraordinary adventures, he is moulded into a mature young man with a great deal of worldly experience. Furthermore, because of his promise to Kensuke to keep his secret, another ten years go by before he puts the story to paper, giving him even more time to grow and develop. Once this time has passed, Michael decides to make this secret common knowledge, because "I want the world to know him as I knew him" (p. 2).

Although their relationship gets off to a rocky start, the two protagonists then spend some time getting to know each other and getting used to each other's quirks. For example, Kensuke teaches Michael how to fish and paint shells, which brings the two characters much closer together. In return, Michael teaches him English and about the technological advances of the modern world, and Kensuke also tells him a bit about Japan and its history.

As a writer of children's fiction, Morpurgo's aim was presumably to make his readers think about themes such as friendship, nature, the environment and sustainable development, reflecting his belief that people must learn from others and from the world around them in order to improve themselves.

FURTHER REFLECTION

SOME QUESTIONS TO THINK ABOUT...

- Michael and Kensuke have a particularly strong relationship, but both also want to be reunited with their families. How do they express this pain in the novel?

- Kensuke and Michael view their friendship differently: while Kensuke has become extremely attached to the island over the decades he has lived there and wants Michael to stay there with him, Michael's first priority is still to find his parents. How does the author address this possessiveness through the narrative? Does it stem from jealousy, in your opinion?

- Misfortune is one of the inevitabilities of life, as the novel explores through the redundancy letter and the storm. Although these events are essentially negative in nature, the protagonists are able to turn them to their advantage. Give a third example of a negative occurrence in the story that turns out to have a hidden benefit.

- Michael studies nature throughout his adventure, both on the sailboat and on the island. In your opinion, how will the knowledge he has gained be of use to him in his adult life?
- Kensuke learns English from Michael, but does not teach his young friend Japanese in return. Why do you think this is?
- Analyse the ways that the author reveals Kensuke's character and backstory over the course of the novel.
- Michael was sworn to silence about his friend's existence for an entire decade. What do you think it would have been most difficult for him to stay quiet about?
- How do you think Kensuke felt after Michael left?
- Which animals do you think the poachers were most interested in?
- Describe the role the football plays in the novel.

We want to hear from you!
Leave a comment on your online library
and share your favourite books on social media!

FURTHER READING

REFERENCE EDITION

- Morpurgo, M. (2003) *Kensuke's Kingdom*. New York: Scholastic Press.

MORE FROM BRIGHTSUMMARIES.COM

- Reading guide – *War Horse* by Michael Morpurgo.

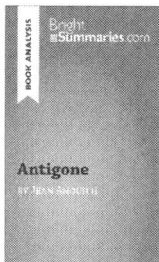

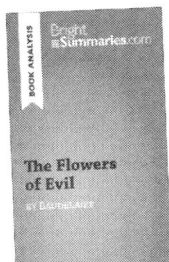

www.brightsummaries.com

Ebook EAN: 9782808010740

Paperback EAN: 9782808010757

Legal Deposit: D/2018/12603/275

This guide was written with the collaboration of
Tina Van Roeyen for the sections "Finding a home in
nature" and "A coming-of-age novel".

Cover: © Primento

Digital conception by Primento, the digital partner of
publishers.

Printed in Great Britain
by Amazon